The

Flat Coated Retriever

– A Complete Anthology of the Dog –

1870-1940

ISBN No.
978-14455-2603-4 (Paperback)
978-14455-2723-9 (Hardback)

British Library Cataloguing-in-Publication Data
A catalogue record for this book is available from
the British Library

VDB

www.vintagedogbooks.com

Contents

Containing chapters from the following sources:

FLAT - COATED RETRIEVER.

THE FLAT OR WAVY COATED BLACK RETRIEVER.

THIS handsome and kindly animal, so say its admirers, is to be the sporting dog of the future. Whether this will prove the case or not only that future can decide, but, taking a line from the progress it has made in public esteem during the past dozen years or so, it is a prognostication likely enough to prove correct. Here we have a creature made for use; handsome, kindly in disposition, obedient, easy to rear, breeding true to type, and well answering the purpose for which it is intended, so there can be little fear of retrogression on its part. Though the curly-coated dog had obtained the advantage at the start, he is coming in but a very bad second. The causes of this have already been alluded to.

The flat or wavy coated retriever is now pretty well distributed throughout the British Isles, and few shooting parties leave home unaccompanied by a well trained specimen or two, which are, however,

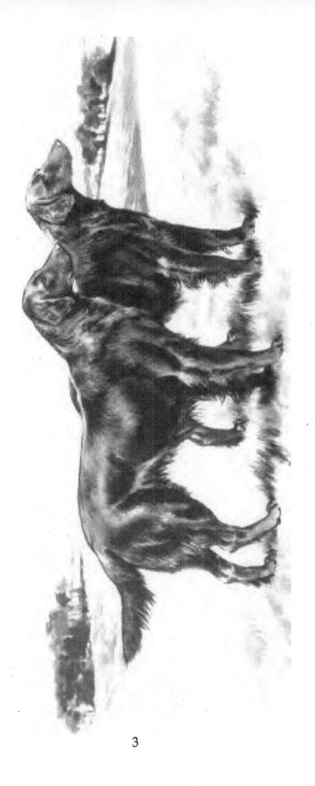

3

actually more useful in turnips and on comparatively open ground, than they are in thick covert and tangled brushwood. Their coats are fine, and certainly not made for the purpose of resisting thorns and briers, and, so far as the experience of the writer goes, their one fault lies in their indisposition to face thick covert, and in whins and gorse I have seen them actually useless. Still, I have been told that there are some strains that I believe will do as well in the roughest covert as the curly dog. A friend of mine was taking exception to the lack of perseverance a flat-coated retriever displayed in making out the line of a winged pheasant that had run about some bramble bushes; at the same time praising his own dog, with a curly coat on him as shaggy as that of a Herdwick sheep. There requires to be a happy mean between the two, for, where one would not face the brambles at all, the other would, and had to be cut out of them, the strong prickles holding him fast as if he were in a net. On the conclusion of each day's shooting it would take two or three hours to free my friend's dog from the "burrs" that had become entangled in his coat. A hard, wavy coated retriever, clad in a jacket not unlike those possessed by the German griffons, would be useful in a rough country.

The first introduction of the flat-coated retriever

to the show bench was at Cremorne in 1873, but in the first volume of the Kennel Club Stud Book, printed in 1874, the two varieties are classed together. He was a much bigger and coarser dog than he is now. Some of the early specimens were pure and simple little Newfoundlands, and it has taken a few years' careful work to bring the wavy retriever to what it is at the present time. Not too big but just big enough. Our grandfathers said, "Oh! we want a big retriever, a strong 'un; one that can jump a gate with an 8lb. hare in its mouth, and gallop with one at full speed." This is not so now. A comparatively small dog is well able to carry a hare, and shooting is so precise that puss does not run as far as she did, when properly hit. Dogs are not made to assist bad shooters to fill a bag; and a man who cannot, in ninety-nine cases out of a hundred, stop a hare before she has run seventy yards, ought not to fire at another. And you do not require to have a special dog for that one chance in a hundred.

Such animals as Dr. Bond Moore used to show were of enormous size and coarse to boot, and I am sure would not be looked at in the show ring to-day. If any of the blood of this strain remains it must be in very small quantities. One or two of his dogs had ugly light eyes, which, objectionable as it may be in other dark-coloured dogs, is more than trebly so in a retriever. The two Wyndhams which came earlier were better dogs, especially Mr. Meyrick's, that was winning at the leading shows from 1864 to 1870. Mr. W. Brailsford brought out the other Wyndham, this in 1860, a dog which was evidently almost pure Labrador, and, like its name-sake, has no pedigree in the Stud Book. Still, both dogs were successful on the show bench, so were much used, and their blood is to be found in most of the strains at the present day. Another excellent dog of the earlier period was Major Allison's Victor, which he had purchased at Edinburgh, and he, too, was without a pedigree so far as could be ascertained, and partook more of the Labrador character than that of the modern strains. It is interesting to note how true to type these pedigreeless dogs have proved, and do so at the present time. For instance, Mr. L. A. Shuter, of near Farningham, in Kent, some time ago purchased a bitch in the streets at Bristol, and could not obtain the slightest trace as to what her sire and dam were. Still, so good was she that he formed an alliance between her and his dog Darenth. The result was puppies so good that they won prizes in keen competition directly they came to be shown. Such cases are, however, exceptional, and must not be considered when mentioned here as an indication that I do not value pedigree, because the contrary is the case, and I would never have allowed any pedigreeless dog to be entered in the Kennel Club Stud Book.

To Mr. S. E. Shirley, the president of the Kennel Club, the admirers of the wavy-coated retrievers are indebted for what he has done for the popularisation of the breed, and most of all the best dogs of the present day are of his strain. A valued lot of retrievers had been kept at Ettington Park long before the dogs of the show bench, and Mr. Shirley remembers black retrievers in the kennels there more than forty years ago. These dogs were much wavier in the coat than is the present fashion. In addition to those at Ettington Park, in the time of the father of the present popular owner, the neighbouring gentry round about Stratford-on-Avon had strains of their own, and these the late Mr. Shirley made use of in founding his kennel. One dog in these early days was especially valued, for he excelled all others in work as well as in looks. This was Nep, who belonged to Wey, then head keeper to Captain Peach, of Idlecote. The dog was, however, too valuable to stay long with his breeder, and Wey sold him for £20, a very high price then, to the late Mr. West, of Alscot Park. In due course Nep was the sire of a dog called Moses, who will no doubt be recollected by retriever breeders as the father of Mr. J. D. Gorse's once well known Sailor.

The blood of this dog still remains in the best dogs in Mr. Shirley's kennels, and it is more than thirty years since he began to give special attention to improving the retriever for show purposes. This he did by purchasing and using the best dogs obtainable, and by careful selection got them to the uniformity of type and general excellence as they are seen to-day on the benches at Birmingham and elsewhere. No setter cross has ever been used, but one of the older stock, Paris, was a Labrador, still he was a great winner on the bench in his day. Mr. G. T. Bartram's good old dog, Zelstone, used with great success up to the time of his death as a sire, had likewise an undoubted strain of Labrador in him.

I have entered into the particulars of this kennel pretty fully for two reasons—because it is one of the most important at present, and that from which almost all others have sprung, and, secondly, because it has been previously stated that Mr. Shirley's retrievers were purely and simply crosses from the Labrador. That they have but a slight tinge of that breed in them, and are mainly indebted for their excellence to careful selection from old local strains, is very evident from what I have written.

Lieut.-Colonel Cornwall Legh, near Knutsford, also owns a considerable kennel of a strain that have proved themselves equally acceptable as workers as on the show bench. Mr. H. Liddell, Otterburn Hall, Northumberland; Mr. John Morrison, Standeford, near Wolverhampton; Mr. C. A. Phillips, Eccles, Lancashire; Mr. G. T. Bartram, of Braintree, whose Zelstone is alluded to above; the Rev. W. Serjeantson, Acton Burnell; Mr. Harding Cox; Mr. L. A. Shuter, Kent; Mr. H. L. Grainger, Northumberland; Mr. H. R. Cooke, Nantwich; Mr. C. C. Hulkes, Sevenoaks; Mr. A. B. F. Mitford, C.B., Moreton on the Marsh; Mr. P. A. Beck, Welshpool; Sir H. de Trafford, Patricroft; Mr. R. P. Meyrick, Wellington, Salop; Mr. G. R. Davies, Cheshire; and Lieut.-Colonel Cotes, Shropshire, have at one time or another possessed, or still possess, capital specimens of the race, some of them owning dogs and bitches in sufficient numbers to perpetuate the breed should any virulent disease attack and destroy all that others own.

A good retriever, handsome in appearance and steady and reliable in work, is to the sportsman a most valuable dog; still he never brings purely fancy prices like many far less useful animals. For instance, we seldom hear of them being claimed at our shows for more than £50 apiece, and when, not long ago, a dog of Colonel Cotes' was run up to £60 at Aldridge's, at which price he changed hands, people stared, though those who desired to own him knew what a good dog he was. In 1896 a somewhat sensational sale took place at the same mart, when a number of flat-coated retrievers, from the kennel of Mr. G. R. Davies, of Hartford, Cheshire, realised excellent prices. They were certainly handsome young dogs; they had all been "handled," but could not be said to be absolutely "finished." There were fourteen in number, which realised $380\frac{1}{2}$ guineas; Kismet, a bitch, bringing 50 guineas, and Deacon, a year old dog, 53 guineas; the lowest price being $10\frac{1}{2}$ guineas, and the general average a trifle over 27 guineas.

At the present time there is a tendency to produce the wavy-coated retrievers with an inclination to the type and shape of head possessed by the setters. This is, no doubt, due to the fallacy carried out in breeding for straight coats, which are all very well in their way, attractive enough in the show ring, but thoroughly bad from a workman's point of view. During my somewhat lengthened connection with dog shows I have noticed that, as a rule, the straightest and flattest coated dogs have the greatest tendency to the longer setter-like heads. If breeding for this coat in preference to that of type of head and character is continued, mischief will be done which may not be so easy to remedy as the variety was to be produced in the first instance. I would especially recommend the judges, in dealing with this retriever, to give more credit for the correct type of head than for an actually and perfectly flat coat, not forgetting that the dog was originally "wavy-coated" quite as much as his jacket was straight.

About judging wavy-coated retrievers. At a recent Birmingham show Mr. Lloyd Price had an unusually fine class of dogs before him, which included an animal called Rightaway, which his owner, Mr. Shirley, considered to be one of the best dogs he ever saw. The judge thought otherwise, and gave the chief award to another from the same kennel. The winner was a much more active-looking dog than Rightaway, equally good in coat, head, and expression, and in legs and feet; but he stood a little higher on the legs, and was not so heavy in bone as the favourite of the Kennel Club's President, who should know a good dog if any man does. Still, on this occasion, we endorse the judge's decision in giving first prize to the more active and workmanlike animal, and it is to be hoped that judges will be consistent, and award the leading honours to those dogs that, from appearance, seem most likely to be useful in the field. As I have already stated, coats can be too fine and straight.

The descriptions and points of the wavy-coated black retriever are as follows :

The *nose and jaws* are to be considered from two points of view—first, as to the powers of scent ; and secondly, as to the capacity for carrying a hare or pheasant without risk of damage. For both purposes the jaws should be long, and, for the development of scenting powers, the nose should be wide, the nostrils open, and its end moist and cool; teeth level, and neither overshot nor undershot.

The *skull, ears, and eyes.*—Skull bone wide and flat at the top, with slight furrow down the middle. Brow by no means pronounced, but the skull is not absolutely in a straight line with the nose. The ears must be small, lie close to the head, and set on low, but not hanging down in hound fashion. With regard to the hair on them, it must be short. The eyes should be of medium size, dark in colour, bright, intelligent-looking, and mild in expression, indicating a good temper.

Neck, loins, and back.—Whatever be the breed of dog, his neck should be long enough to allow him to stoop in seeking for the trail. A chumpy neck is especially bad; for, while a little dog may get along on a foot scent with a short neck, a comparatively large and unwieldy dog tries himself terribly by the necessity for crouching in his fast pace.   Loins and back wide, deep, and strong.

The *quarters and stifles* must be muscular, and so formed to enable the retriever to do his work fast enough to please the modern sportsman, with ease to himself; the stifles should be nicely turned.

The *shoulders* should be long and sloping; otherwise, even with a proper length of neck, the dog cannot stoop to a foot scent without fatigue.

The *chest* should be broad as well as deep, with well-developed and well sprung ribs.

Legs, knees, and *hocks.*—When tolerably fast work is to be done by a heavy dog, it is important that these parts should be strong and free from disease in their joints.   Hence the legs must not only be long and muscular, but they must be clean and free from lumber.   The knees should be broad, and the hocks well developed, and clean.

The *feet* are rather larger proportionately than in the setter, but they should be compact, and the toes well arched.   Soles thick and strong.

The *tail* should be bushy in proportion to the dog,

but not feathered. It should be carried gaily, but not curled over the back.

The *coat* is short, but not so short as in the pointer or hound; it should be close and thick and as straight as possible; a thin open coat, underneath which the skin is easily found, is bad, however straight it may be.

The *colour* should be a rich black, free from rustiness and from white.

Symmetry and temperament.—The symmetry and elegance of this dog are considerable, and should be valued highly. The evidences of good temper must be regarded with great care, since his utility mainly depends on his disposition. A sour-headed brute, with a vicious look about the eyes, should be disqualified.

Weight from 50lb. to 68lb. for dogs; bitches rather smaller.

	Value.		Value.
Nose and jaws	5	Feet	10
Skull, ears, and eyes	10	Tail	5
Neck, loins, and back	10	Coat	10
Quarters and stifles	5	Symmetry and tempera-	
Shoulders and chest	13	ment	20
Legs, knees, and hocks	12		
	—		—
	55		45

Grand Total 100.

Little more is to be said about the flat-coated black retriever, and I can only reiterate that a specimen from a good strain is the best all round dog a man can have for shooting purposes. Well trained, he is thoroughly reliable and absolutely steady when he is kept for retrieving only; but it must not be forgotten that as used by what is generally known as " a one dog man," when he has to hunt and find his game as well as retrieve it, he is not likely to be so absolutely steady as when broken for the one department alone. In choosing such a dog, the colour of eyes and expression ought to be considered, as light coloured eyes, hard features, if they may be so called, and a generally unpleasant outlook, in nine cases out of ten denote an unamiable disposition, bad temper, and that which usually accompanies such defects, a hard mouth. Most retrievers are liable to become hard mouthed at three or four years old, especially when they have worked much amongst rabbits and hares, the reason being that the latter, usually strong and powerful, scratch or otherwise irritate the dog, who to stop them gives just a quiet nip. A sensible dog sooner than a foolish one gets to do this, because it is for his own comfort, and when the bad habit has once been acquired it is not to be cured, and is soon brought to bear on feather as well as on fur. In no case should a retriever be allowed to kill rats or other vermin, as this is another method by which he gets to know that his teeth are given him for biting purposes. However, the training of the retriever may well be left for another volume.

(From *Modern Dogs.*)

THE RETRIEVER (BLACK, FLAT- OR WAVY-COATED).

ORIGIN AND USES same as the black, curly-coated variety.

SCALE OF POINTS, ETC.

	Value.		Value.
Skull	10	Legs, knees, and hocks .	10
Nose and jaws . . .	10	Feet	5
Ears and eyes . . .	5	Tail	5
Neck	5	Coat	5
Loins and back . . .	10	Color	5
Quarters and stifles . .	10	Symmetry and temperament .	10
Shoulders	6		
Chest	4	Total . . .	100

HEAD.—Bone at top wide and flat, with furrow down middle; brows not pronounced. Ears small, set low, carried close to head (not hound-like), covered with short hair. Eyes medium size, dark, mild, and intelligent. Nose wide; nostrils open. Jaws strong and long. Teeth level.

NECK.—Long enough to allow dog to stoop when trailing; loins and back wide, deep, and strong.

QUARTERS AND STIFLES.—Muscular quarters, with nicely turned stifles.

SHOULDERS AND CHEST.—Shoulders long, sloping; chest deep and broad; ribs well sprung.

LEGS AND FEET.—Legs strong, long, and muscular, clean, and free from lumber; knees broad; hocks well developed and clean. Feet rather large, compact, with well-arched toes; soles thick and strong.

TAIL.—Bushy (not feathery); carried gaily, but not over back.

COAT.—Not so short as the pointer's, close, thick, and straight as possible.

COLOR.—Rich black, free from rustiness and white.

SYMMETRY.—Highly valued, likewise evidence of good temper.

WEIGHT.—Dogs, 50 to 70 pounds; bitches smaller.

Mr. Clarence H. Mackay's (253 Broadway, New York City)
"Scrutton Belle"

THE FLAT OR WAVY-COATED BLACK RETRIEVER

Origin and uses are the same as the black, curly-coated variety.

Skull, Eyes and Ears.—Skull bone wide and flat at the top, with slight furrow down the middle. Brow by no means pronounced, but the skull is not absolutely in a straight line with the nose. The ears must be small, lie close to the head, set on low, but not hanging down in hound fashion. With regard to the hair on them, it must be short. The eyes should be of medium size, dark in color, bright, intelligent looking and mild in expression, indicating a good temper.

Nose and Jaws.—These are to be considered from two points of view—first, as to the powers of scent, and secondly, as to the capacity of carrying a hare or pheasant without risk of damage. For both purposes the jaws should be long, and for the development of scenting powers, the nose should be wide, the nostrils open, and its end moist and cool; teeth level and neither overshot nor undershot.

Neck, Back and Loins.—Whatever be the breed of dog, his neck should be long enough to allow him to stoop in seeking the trail. A chumpy neck is especially bad; for, while a little dog may get along on a foot scent with a short neck, a comparatively large and unwieldy dog tries himself terribly by the necessity of crouching in his fast pace. Loins and back wide, deep and strong.

19

Quarters and Stifles.—These must be muscular, and so formed to enable the retriever to do his work fast enough to please the modern sportsman, with ease to himself. The stifles should be nicely turned.

Shoulders.—Should be long and sloping; otherwise, even with a proper length of neck, the dog cannot stoop to a foot scent without fatigue.

Chest.—Broad as well as deep, with well developed and well sprung ribs.

Legs, Knees and Hocks.—When tolerably fast work is to be done by a heavy dog, it is important that these parts should be strong and free from disease in the joints. Hence the legs must not only be long and muscular, but they must be clean and free from lumber. The knees should be broad, and the hocks well developed and clean.

Mr. Harding Cox's (Cassiobridge, Watford, Herts, Eng.)
" Black Drake "

Feet.—Are rather larger proportionately than in the setter, but they should be compact and the toes well arched; soles thick and strong.

Tail.—This should be bushy in proportion to the dog, but not feathered. It should be carried gaily, but not curled over the back.

Coat.—Short, but not so short as in the pointer or hound; it should be close, thick and as straight as possible; a thin open coat, underneath which the skin is easily found, is bad however straight it may be.

Color.—A rich black, free from rustiness and white.

Symmetry and Temperament. —The symmetry and elegance of this dog are considerable, and should be highly valued. The evidences of good temper must be regarded with great care, since his utility mainly depends on his disposition. A sour-headed brute, with a vicious look about the eyes, should be disqualified.

Weight.—From 50 lbs. to 68 lbs. for dogs; bitches rather smaller.

SCALE OF POINTS.

Skull, eyes and ears	10	Legs, knees and hocks	12
Nose and jaws	5	Feet	10
Neck, loins and back	10	Tail	5
Quarters and stifles	5	Coat	10
Shoulders and chest	13	Symmetry and temperament	20

Total 100

COMMENTS.

As a retriever is but very little used in this country, few are ever seen on the bench at any of our shows, fewest of all the curly coated specimen. In comparing the standards of the curly and the flat coated retriever there will be found to exist but little difference, except in the matter of the coat and its quality. In neither of these breeds should there be any semblance of coarseness in any of its features, nor should either have a stop or be built on the lines of the setter, the latter a fault which many dogs possess. All the fanciers of these two breeds desire to eliminate the setter type wholly, if possible, and so pay really more attention to the type of the head than to that of the coat. As these dogs are frequently called upon to retrieve heavy game, they should have good, strong jaws, level teeth, strong neck without coarseness, powerful legs and feet as near perfect as possible. As many a fence has to be taken perhaps with a retrieved hare, good bone and a strong back are essentials. The quality and color of the eye as called for in the standard should be insisted upon.

21

LIEUT.-COLONEL LEGH'S FLAT-COATED RETRIEVER PIRATE

LIEUT.-COLONEL LEGH'S FLAT-COATED RETRIEVER CHAMPION TWIDDLE

TEAM OF MR. E. W. H. BLAGG'S RETRIEVERS.
BROKEN TO THE TAME RABBIT.

I.—THE FLAT-COATED RETRIEVER.

BY L. P. C. ASTLEY.

IT is obviously useless to shoot game unless you can find it after it has been wounded or killed, and from the earliest times it has been the habit of sportsmen to train their dogs to do the work which they could not always successfully do for themselves. The Pointers, Setters, and Spaniels of our forefathers were carefully broken not only to find and stand their game, but also to fetch the fallen birds. This use of the setting and pointing dog is still common on the Continent and in the United States, and there is no inaccuracy in a French artist depicting a Pointer with a partridge in its mouth, or showing a Setter retrieving waterfowl. In the time of Morland and Cooper it was equally correct in English art, and the Setter or Spaniel was considered quite normal if after the shot had been fired he found the wounded bird, and laid it crushed and mangled at his master's feet.

The Springer and the old curly-coated water-dog were regarded as particularly adroit in the double work of finding and retrieving. Pointers and Setters who had been thus broken were found to deteriorate in steadiness in the field, and it gradually came to be realised that even the Spaniel's capacity for retrieving was limited. A larger and quicker dog was wanted to divide the labour, and to be used solely as a retriever in conjunction with the other gun dogs. The Poodle was tried for retrieving with some success, and he showed considerable aptitude in finding and fetching wounded wild duck; but he, too, was inclined to maul his birds and deliver them dead.

Even the Old English Sheepdog was occasionally engaged in the work, and various crosses with Spaniel or Setter and Collie were attempted in the endeavour to produce a grade breed having the desired qualities of a good nose, a soft mouth, and an understanding brain, together with a coat that would protect its wearer from the ill effects of frequent immersion in water.

It was when these efforts were most

active—namely about the year 1850—that new material was discovered in a black-coated dog recently introduced into England from Labrador. He was a natural water-dog, with a constitution impervious to chills, and entirely free from the liability to ear canker, which had always been a drawback to the use of the Spaniel as a retriever of waterfowl. Moreover, he was himself reputed to be a born retriever of game, and remarkably sagacious. His importers called him a Spaniel—a breed name which at one time was also applied to his relative the Newfoundland. Probably there were not many specimens of the race in England, and, although there is no record explicitly saying so, it is conjectured that these were crossed with the English Setter, producing what is now familiarly known as the black, flat-coated Retriever.

One very remarkable attribute of the Retriever is that notwithstanding the known fact that the parent stock was mongrel, and that in the early dogs the Setter type largely predominated, the ultimate result has favoured the Labrador cross distinctly and prominently, proving how potent, even when grafted upon a stock admittedly various, is the blood of a pure race, and how powerful its influence for fixing type and character over the other less vital elements with which it is blended.

From the first, sportsmen recognised the extreme value of the new retrieving dog. Strengthened and improved by the Labrador blood, he had lost little if any of the Setter beauty of form. He was a dignified, substantial, intelligent, good-tempered, affectionate companion, faithful, talented, highly cultivated, and esteemed, in the season and out of it, for his mind as well as his beauty.

" Idstone " described one of the early Retrievers, and the description is worth quoting :—

" He was black as a raven—a blue black—not a very large dog, but wide over the back and loins, with limbs like a lion, and a thick, glossy, long, silky coat, which parted down the back, a long, sagacious head, full of character and clean as a Setter's in the matter of coat. His ears were small, and so close to his head

that they were hidden in his feathered neck. His eye was neither more nor less than a human eye, and I never saw a bad expression in it. He was not over twenty-five inches in height, but he carried a hare with ease ; and if he could not top a gate with one—which about one dog in two hundred does twice a year—he could get through the second or third span, or push it through a gap before him in his mouth, and never lose his hold. And then for water. He would trot into the launching punt, and coil himself up by the luncheon basket to wait for his master as soon as he saw the usual preparations for a cruise. For this work he had too much coat, and brought a quantity of water into the boat ; but for retrieving wildfowl he was excellent ; and in the narrow water-courses and amongst the reeds and osiers his chase of a winged mallard was a thing to see. They seemed both to belong to one element, and he would dive like an otter for yards, sometimes coming up for breath, only to go down again for pleasure."

It is only comparatively recently that we have realised how excellent an all-round sporting dog the Retriever has become. In many cases, indeed, where grouse and partridge are driven or walked-up a well-broken, soft-mouthed Retriever is unquestionably superior to Pointer, Setter, or Spaniel, and for general work in the field he is the best companion that a shooting man can possess.

Doubtless in earlier days, when the art of training was less thoroughly understood, the breaking of a dog was a matter of infinite trouble to breeders. Most of the gun dogs could be taught by patience and practice to retrieve fur or feather, but game carefully and skilfully shot is easily rendered valueless by being mumbled and mauled by powerful jaws not schooled to gentleness. And this question of a tender mouth was certainly one of the problems that perturbed the minds of the originators of the breed. The difficulty was overcome by a process of selection, and by the exclusion from breeding operations of all hard-mouthed specimens, with the happy effect that in the present time it is exceptional to find a working Retriever who does not know how to bring his bird to hand without injuring it. A better knowledge of what is expected of him distinguishes our modern Retriever. He knows his duty, and is intensely eager to perform it, but he no longer rushes off unbidden at the firing of the gun. He has learned to remain at heel until he is ordered by word or gesture from his master, upon whom he relies as his friend and director, and " who to him is instead of a god."

It would be idle to expect that the offspring of unbroken sire and dam can be as

him very early to enter water, or he may be found wanting when you require him to fetch a bird from river or lake. Lessons in retrieving ought to be a part of his daily routine. Equally necessary is it to break him in to the knowledge that sheep and lambs are not game to be chased, and that rabbits and hares are to be discriminated from feathered game. Mr. Blagg trains his Retrievers to steadiness with " fur " by schooling them to harmless companionship with tame rabbits.

MR. H. REGINALD COOKE'S **CH. WORSLEY BESS.**
FROM THE PAINTING BY MAUD EARL.

Gun - shyness is often supposed to be hereditary; but it is not so. Any puppy can be cured of gun-shyness in half a dozen short lessons. Sir Henry Smith's advice is to get your puppy accustomed to the sound and sight of a gun being fired, first at a distance and gradually nearer and nearer, until he knows that no harm will come to him. Associate the gun-firing in his

easily educated as a Retriever whose parents before him have been properly trained. Inherited qualities count for a great deal in the adaptability of all sporting dogs, and the reason why one meets with so many Retrievers that are incapable or disobedient or gun-shy is simply that their preliminary education has been neglected — the education which should begin when the dog is very young.

In his earliest youth he should be trained to prompt obedience to a given word or a wave of the hand. It is well to teach

mind with something pleasant—as a sign that it is feeding time, or time for a free romp in the paddock. There is no more reason that a dog should fear a gun than that he should fear the cracking of a whip. Companionship and sympathy between dog and master is the beginning and end of the whole business, and there is a moral obligation between them which ought never to be strained.

No breed of sporting dog has gained more than the Retriever from the institution of that admirable organisation the Game-keepers' Association, and from the well-conducted shows for keepers' dogs managed by Mr. Millard. At the Gamekeepers' Show held at Carlisle in 1907 visitors were particularly attracted by the high quality of the exhibits in the Retriever classes, all owned and most of them bred by keepers.

As a show dog the flat-coated Retriever has reached something very near to the ideal standard of perfection which has been consistently bred up to. Careful selection and systematic breeding, backed up by enthusiasm, have resulted in the production of a dog combining useful working qualities with the highest degree of beauty.

In the early days of dog shows the one name most intimately associated with the Retriever was that of Dr. Bond Moore, whose kennels were almost invariably successful in competition. Dr. Moore was somewhat arbitrary as a judge of the breed, and has been known to fault an otherwise perfect dog because of the presence of a few white hairs in its jet black coat; but it is interesting to note that in the litters of his own breeding at Wolverhampton there occasionally occurred puppies of a pale golden, almost liver colour. His famous Midnight, remarkable for the pure blackness of her coat, more than once threw sandy-coloured whelps to a black sire. This occurs in many good strains.

Contemporaneously with the success of Dr. Moore's kennels in 1870 some admirably typical Retrievers were shown by other breeders, notably Mr. Atkinson's Cato, Mr. Shorthose's Rupert, Mr. Strawbridge's Rose, Mr. Hazlehurst's Midnight, Mr. G. D. Gorse's Wyndham, Sailor, and Jet, Mr. R. J. Lloyd Price's Moliere, and Mr. G. Manson's Morley. Another very prominent admirer and breeder was the late Mr. S. E. Shirley, the President of the Kennel Club, who owned many Retrievers superlative both as workers and as show dogs, and who probably did more for the breed than any other man of his

MR. H. REGINALD COOKE'S CH. WIMPOLE PETER.
FROM THE PAINTING BY MAUD EARL.

generation. A sportsman in every sense, Mr. Shirley trained his dogs for work with extreme care, and only bred from those of the highest character. If only for his improvements in this one breed, the shooting world owes his memory undying gratitude. Among the best Retrievers of his breeding were Paris, Moonstone, Zelstone, Dusk, Lady Evelyn, Trace, and Thorn.

Mr. Shirley's work was carried on by Mr. Harding Cox, who devoted much time and energy to the production of good Retrievers, many of which were of Mr. Shirley's strain. Mr. Cox's dogs deservedly achieved con-

27

siderable fame for their levelness of type, and the improvement in heads so noticeable at the present time is to be ascribed to his breeding for this point. Mr. L. Allen Shuter, the owner of Ch. Darenth and other excellent

MR. A. H. HORSMAN'S CH. SHOTOVER
BY CH. BLACK QUILT——QUEEN OF LLANGOLLEN.

Retrievers of his own breeding, claims also a large share of credit for the part he has played in the general improvement of the breed. Mr. C. A. Phillips, too, owned admirable specimens in Ch. Taut and other good workers, and the name of the late Lieut.-Colonel Cornwall Legh must be included. Many of Colonel Legh's bitches were of Shirley blood, but it is believed that a breed of Retrievers had existed at High Legh for several generations, with which a judicious cross was made, the result being not only the formation of a remarkable kennel, but also a decided influence for good upon the breed in general.

But since the Shirley days, when competition was more limited than it is at present, no kennel of Retrievers has ever attained anything like the distinction of that owned by Mr. H. Reginald Cooke, at Riverside, Nantwich. By acquiring the best specimens of the breed from all available sources, Mr. Cooke has gathered together a stock which has never been equalled. His ideas of type and conformation are the outcome of close and attentive study and consistent practice, and one needs to go to Riverside if one desires to see the highest examples of what a modern flat-coated Retriever can be. Within recent years Mr. Cooke has owned Ch. Black Quilt (perhaps the most successful sire of the race), Paul of Riverside, Worsley Bess, Gipsy of Riverside, Ch. High Legh Blarney, and Ch. Wimpole Peter, and at the present moment the Riverside kennels contain ten champions in addition to many potential champions.

Since Dr. Bond Moore imparted to the Retriever a fixity of character, the coats have become longer and less wavy, and in conformation of skull, colour of eye, straightness of legs, and quality of bone, there has been a perceptible improvement.

As there is no club devoted to the breed, and consequently no official standard of points, the following description of the perfect Retriever is offered.

MR. E. W. H. BLAGG'S BUSY MITE
BY CH. WIMPOLE PETER——STYLISH QUEEN.
Photograph by Lowndes, Cheadle.

1. **General Appearance.**—That of a well-proportioned bright and active sporting dog, showing power without lumber and raciness without weediness.

2. **Head.**—Long, fine, without being weak, the

28

muzzle square, the underjaw strong with an absence of lippiness or throatiness.

3. Eyes.—Dark as possible, with a very intelligent, mild expression.

4. Neck.—Long and clean.

5. Ears.—Small, well set on, and carried close to the head.

6. Shoulders.—Oblique, running well into the back, with plenty of depth of chest.

7. Body.—Short and square, and well ribbed up.

8. Stern.—Short and straight, and carried gaily, but not curled over the back.

9. Forelegs.—Straight, pasterns strong, feet small and round.

10. Quarters.—Strong ; stifles well bent.

11. Coat.—Dense black or liver, of fine quality and texture. Flat, not wavy.

12. Weight.—From 65 lb. to 80 lb. for dogs ; bitches rather less.

As a rule the Retriever should be chosen for the intelligent look of his face, and particular attention should be paid to the shape of his head and to his eyes. His frame is important, of course, but in the Retriever the mental qualities are of more significance than bodily points.

There has been a tendency in recent years among Retriever breeders to fall into the common error of exaggerating a particular point, and of breeding dogs with a head far too fine and narrow—it is what has been aptly called the alligator head—lacking in brain capacity and power of jaw. A perfect head should be long and clean, but ne ther weak nor snipy. The eye should be placed just halfway between the occiput and the tip of the nose.

It is pleasing to add that to this beautiful breed the phrase " handsome is as handsome does " applies in full measure. Not only is the average Retriever of a companionable disposition, with delightful intelligence that is always responsive, but he is a good and faithful guard and a courageous protector of person and property. It has already been said that the majority of the best-looking Retrievers are also good working dogs, and it may here be added that many of the most successful working dogs are sired by prizewinners in the show ring. At the late Retriever trials at St. Neots the open stake was won by Mr. Reginald Cooke's Ch. Grouse of Riverside, a son of Mr. Allen Shuter's Ch. Horton Rector. Ch. Royal River and Ch. Shotover were also successful runners at the Kennel Club trials at Horsted who helped to prove that the show dog need not necessarily be deficient in the capacity to excel as a worker.

29

The Flat-Coated Retriever.

This variety commenced its career at about the same date that the Curly-coated Retriever was becoming recognised, or at any rate, a short time afterwards. To the late Mr. S. E. Shirley (of Ettington Park) has always been attached the credit of having originated and produced Flat-coated Retrievers. To a certain extent this is true, as Mr. Shirley very keenly took them up in their infancy, fixed a scale of Show points, and eventually founded a kennel of Flat-coated Retrievers, which had a world-wide reputation. Yet it is only fair to say, that the *original strain*, from which these dogs have all been bred, can be traced back to a working strain of Retriever owned by J. D. Hull, at one time keeper to Mr. J. H. Whitehouse (of Redditch). The writer is unable to obtain any authenticated information regarding the origin of Hull's dogs, except that he was one of the early breeders of a dog for *retrieving only*, and it is more than probable that he employed a Setter cross, which gave the wavy,—and later still,—straight coats. It is not until a bitch named "Boss" appeared upon the scene, that anything definite can be stated. In 1862, this bitch was mated with a dog named "Black Sailor," belonging to Mr. Blaydon, and among the progeny was a bitch eventually christened "Old Bounce." Mr. William Lort—of Setter fame—advised Hull to put "Old Bounce" to Mr. H. Cattock's "Cato" (whose breeding cannot be traced), and the result of this union in 1865 was "Young Bounce," and another bitch, known in K.C.S.B. (Vol. I.) as Mr. T. D. Richardson's "Belle." The Rev. W. Serjeantson (of Acton Burnell Rectory) writes :—" 'Old Bounce' and 'Young Bounce' were very like one another, a trifle 'on the leg,' but as good in coat as most of the present-day Retrievers, and both had long, but *sensible* heads and short ears." In 1871, Mr. Shirley bought a dog named "Paris," which had previously been exhibited by Dr. Bond Moore under the name of "Lion." This animal was by Sir Henry Paulett's imported Labrador "Lion" out of "Bess," also an imported Labrador. "Paris" was a rather big, cobby dog, with flattish, thick coat of fairish length, and he had short ears and a short wedge-shaped head—in fact he was utterly unlike the Labrador of these days. A little later, a bitch named "Lady Evelyn," bred by Mr. R. J. L. Price and also some other bitches of Hull's strain, were added to the Ettington Kennels, whilst in 1874, Mr. Shirley bought a son of "Young Bounce's" named "Bob," whom he re-christened "Thorn." "Thorn" was by "Victor" (pedigree unknown). This latter was a big, handsome, upstanding animal that Colonel Allison had claimed at Edinburgh Show, on account of his working reputation. In the same year, Rev. W. Serjeantson bought another of "Young Bounce's" puppies—a bitch named "Midnight," by Sir Thomas Meyrick's "Wyndham." "Wyndham" was a big, compact, "merry" dog, bred by Captain Sparling (of Petton), but again unfortunately his pedigree has not been preserved. Mr. Serjeantson, who often saw "Wyndham" at work, says—"I once asked Captain Sparling about 'Wyndham's' breeding, but he knew nothing about it. I have always thought that he came from Hawkstone, which is not far from Petton, because, in 1862, Sir F. Smythe (of Acton Burnell) had a dog from Hawkstone, which to my mind was evidently of the same strain, and Retrievers in those days, did not all bear the same family likeness, that they do now." "Midnight" was a very good-looking bitch, with a rather wavy coat, and she was also a well-broken and first-rate Retriever in the field. In the hands of Mr. Shirley, Rev. W. Serjeantson, and Colonel Cotes [who all began breeding Flat-coated Retrievers about the same time] steady progress was made, and although, as time went on, other strains crept in, yet undoubtedly all Flat-coated Retrievers go back to Hull's kennel, and the "Bounce" blood can be found in practically

31

every pedigree of the present day. At this period, the
coats of many Retrievers had a decided "wave," in fact
they were originally described as Wavy-coated Retrievers.
The origin of a really flat, straight coat, can be traced to
Mr. Bartram's "Zelstone," a small, cobby, good-looking
dog, bred by Mr. Farquharson (of Blandford) and whom
Mr. Shirley crossed with his bitch "Think." This cross
was wonderfully successful as regards looks, but although
"Zelstone" gave the breed flat coats and greater docility,
yet to him some of the older breeders ascribe the origin of
the listlessness and slackness, so prevalent in Retrievers
now-a-days. A glance at "Think's" pedigree will give the
reader a better idea of early breeding than any written
description, and the writer therefore inserts it.

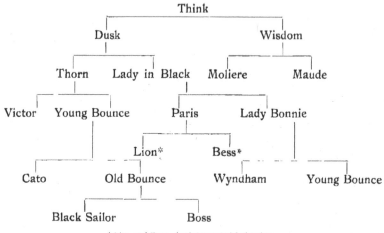

* Lion and Bess—both Imported Labradors.

It is not within the scope of this article to name many
of the distinguished Show bench Retrievers that appeared
before the public during the next decade, so the following
names and descriptions must suffice. "Moonstone," (by
"Zelstone"—"Think"), a large and very handsome Retriever
with a good deal of coat. "Hopeful, (by "Harvester"—
"Think"), and, again, his son "Heedful," were very

successful as prize winners and sires of prize winners.
"Rightaway," (by "Frank"—"Amesbury Trace"), who was
a coarse-looking dog, and "Wiseacre" (another "Zelstone"
—"Think" produce), a handsome animal of workmanlike
type, were also big winners at the leading Shows. Other
notable Retrievers about this time were "Tedworth Wave"

MR. H. R. COOKE'S WORSLEY BESS.
From a Painting by Maud Earl.

(a litter sister to "Rightaway,") a big, bony bitch shewing
considerable character. "Breeze" (by "Ben"—"Flirt"), a
most successful brood bitch, especially when mated with
"Moonstone." "Mahdi" and "Miner," good-looking dogs on
the large side, and the result of the "Moonstone"—"Breeze"
union. And lastly, a bitch named "Lady in Black," whose
name crops up very frequently in Retriever pedigrees.

Naturally, as time went on, fresh breeders sprang into existence, and the Flat- or Wavy-coated Retriever was no longer in the hands of a few men only. Among a somewhat lengthy list of prominent owners and breeders during the last twenty-five years, it will be sufficient, in addition to those already named, to mention the following:—

MR. H. R. COOKE'S HIGH LEGH BLARNEY.
From a Painting by Maud Earl.

Lord Redesdale, Colonel Cornwall Legh (a breeder of many prize winners), Messrs. E. G. Farquharson, Harding Cox (who owned at one time a very successful kennel, and was also the breeder of "Black Quilt"), G. Reynolds Davies, L. Allen Shuter, and H. R. Cooke. It is chiefly due to the above owners, that the family of Flat-coats is now so widespread over the United Kingdom, special stress being laid on the last-mentioned name, as the Riverside kennel has easily established a record as regards numbers of winners on the Show bench.

By the time that the nineties were reached, the general appearance of the leading prize winners had become more uniform, although at times judges were found to vary very considerably in their ideas of the type required. But on the whole, the Retrievers exhibited in the nineties were a fairly even lot, with some very handsome dogs standing out prominently from the general crowd.

Mr. H. R. Cooke writes :—

The best-looking dogs and bitches exhibited in the nineties, I take to be as follows, and I place them in merit, in the order that I have written them. *Dogs.*—"Wimpole Peter," "Darenth," "Blizzard," and "Pettings Mallard." The latter had hardly the "class" of the three first-named, but he deserves mention for his wonderful bone, legs and feet. *Bitches.*—"Worsley Bess," "Black Queen," "Talent," and "Etta." I consider that "Worsley Bess" stands out by herself as the most typical Retriever bitch ever seen, either during her career or since, and I take her as my model to breed up to, and have not yet seen a reproduction of her.

The same authority states :—

As regards Retrievers exhibited since 1900, I select the following lot, written in the order of merit. *Dogs.*—"High Legh Blarney," "Rocket of Riverside," "Black Quilt," and "Horton Rector." *Bitches.*—"Judy of Riverside," "High Legh Quito," "Gipsy of Riverside," and "Bank Bess." Of this lot, I think the only ones, that could beat those exhibited in the nineties, are "Blarney" and "Rocket"—the former of whom, is to my mind the best Retriever of either sex that I ever saw, although for a working dog, he is a size too big.

Mr. Cooke modestly adds, that in the above selection he is obliged to mention several Retrievers which he owns or has owned at one time, but as Mr. Cooke has for many years held the strongest kennel of Show Retrievers that have ever been collected together, it is not to be wondered that several of their names are rightly selected. In addition to the above, mention should be made of two animals, whose names occur very frequently in modern pedigrees, namely, Colonel Cornwall Legh's " Taut " and Mr. Harding Cox's "Black Drake." The former was a dog of beautiful quality, but marred by too soft an expression and with a somewhat listless carriage. He was, however, a great success as a sire of prize winning Retrievers, especially when mated with bitches that were lacking in Show quality. "Black Drake," on the other hand, was conspicuous for his bone and great Retriever character, although his type of head prevented him from obtaining highest Show honours; at the same time, he was a beautifully bodied dog, with well-sprung ribs and strong coupling, while most of his stock showed strength and activity.

DESCRIPTION.

A general description of a Flat-coated Retriever—given briefly and nearly in the words of a man who has owned and judged many good specimens—is as follows :—*Head*—Long, fine, without being weak ; muzzle, square ; underjaw, strong, and an absence of lippiness or throatiness. *Eye*—Dark brown, with a very intelligent, mild expression. *Neck*—Long and clean. *Ears*—Small and well set on, carried close to the head. *Shoulders*—Oblique, running well into the back, with plenty of depth of chest. *Body*—Short, square, and well ribbed up. *Stern*—Short and straight, never carried above the level of the back. *Fore-legs*—Straight, pasterns fairly long but strong. *Feet*—Strong but compact. *Quarters*—Strong, and stifles well bent. *Coat*—Dense, black (or liver), of fine quality and texture; flat, not wavy. *General Appearance*—A bright, active dog, showing power without lumber, and raciness without weediness. Weight, 60—70 lbs., as a dog of "medium " size, if properly put together will invariably *kill* the heavy, big dogs, on a hard shooting day.

The above description is what most breeders of Exhibition Flat-coated Retrievers aim to produce, and there is certainly no dog more "taking" in appearance than a good-looking specimen of this breed. During the last few years a bitter controversy has periodically been

waged concerning the general appearance and working capabilities of the present-day Flat-coated Retrievers. Much ink has been used (we dare not say wasted) and much heart-burning caused! The writer has no intention of opening up this subject, beyond merely making a few remarks in as impartial a manner as possible. As regards the appearance of *good* specimens—putting aside entirely the flat-sided and weakly constructed animals that sometimes obtain prizes—there is no reason why the conformation should be changed, provided dogs are not bred *too big*, nor too much stress laid on length of head and its consequent flatness of skull. But undoubtedly there is room for improvement in the working capabilities of the breed, if they are to live up to the reputations that some of their forebears left behind. With Flat-coated Retrievers, it has not been a case of "Advance Australia!" They have reached a certain point, but seem incapable of getting further on the road to perfection, chiefly owing to the old hackneyed cry of "want of nose and dash." The latter, however, is gradually improving, and it now behoves all breeders to turn their attentions more seriously to "nose." This can only be effected by unanimously deciding that working qualities must rank first, and that "handsome impostors" must *never* be allowed to contaminate the breed, no matter what prizes they may have won in the Show ring. That Shows—owing to their increased numbers of late years—have done more harm than good to the working qualities of Retrievers, is urged by many experienced men, and the writer is among those who would hail with delight any scheme, which would allow only proved good workers to obtain prizes on the Bench.*
Another matter, which has been recently pointed out, and rightly so, is the want of fresh blood for an outcross—there being now practically no Retrievers which have not been interbred with the Show strains.

And now, having drawn attention to some of the weak points, let us consider the virtues of the breed. The Flat-coated Retriever may be termed "an amiable dog"—he is almost invariably good tempered and friendly, these qualities thereby making him a very

---

*Since the above was written the Kennel Club has made a rule that no Pointer, Setter, Sporting Spaniel nor Retriever can obtain the title of "Champion" unless, in addition to having been awarded three Challenge Certificates by three different judges, he must also have gained a prize or Certificate of Merit at a Field Trial which is recognised by the Kennel Club. (Gen. Editor.)

easy subject for breaking to the gun.   If bred for practical purposes, and not for Show points alone, he is usually intelligent and willing to learn, is gifted with a tender mouth (a very important factor with Retrievers), and takes to water naturally.   In addition to this, he is generally a fast galloper in his work, a point by no means to be ignored in these days of grouse and partridge driving.

W. G. ELEY.

THE FLAT-COATED RETRIEVER

The Flat-coated Retriever owes its origin to the late Mr. S. E. Shirley of Ettington Park, near Stratford on-Avon. The variety originates about the year 1860, from the setter crossed with a small Newfoundland dog of a different type to the Labrador of to-day.

Far stronger and larger than the Labradors, it is suitable for heavy work such as long days on heavy land, to face stretches of mud and water after fowl. They are most delightful companions to the shooting man. The best for sport are medium sized dogs. Weight 50 to 65 lb. Bitches rather less.

The Flat-coated Retriever is one of the most popular shooting dogs. Its extremely handsome appearance and certainly remarkable working powers has brought the variety well to the front. An excellent study of a bitch with her puppies is shown.

No one can forget the paintings by Maud Earl of Mr. H. Reginald Cook's champions. Apart from the beauty of the picture, the most magnificent examples of this breed are depicted accurately.

FLAT-COATED RETRIEVER, 'Joan of Riverside,' the property of
Mr. H. R. Cooke, Riverside, Nantwich, Cheshire.
The Flat-coated originated about the year 1860, from the Setter crossed
with a small Newfoundland dog.

THE FLAT-COATED RETRIEVER.

Head : Long and nicely moulded. The skull flat and moderately broad. There is a depression or stop between the eyes, slight and in no way accentuated so as to avoid giving either a down or a dish-faced appearance. The nose of good size with open nostrils. The eyes, of medium size, are dark brown or hazel, with a very intelligent expression (a round prominent eye is a disfigurement). The eyes not to be obliquely placed. The jaws long and strong, with a capacity of carrying a hare or pheasant. The ears small and well set on close to the side of the head. The **head** well set in the **neck,** which is long and free from throatiness, symmetrically set and obliquely placed in shoulders, runs well into the back to allow of easily seeking for the trail. The **chest** deep and fairly broad, with a well-defined brisket, on which the elbows work cleanly and evenly. The **fore ribs** fairly flat, showing a gradual spring and well arched in the centre of the body but rather lighter towards the quarters. Open couplings are to be ruthlessly condemned. The **back** short, square and well ribbed up, with muscular quarters. The **stern** short, straight and well set on, carried gaily but never much above the level of the back. **Legs and Feet :** These are of the greatest importance. The **forelegs** should be perfectly straight, with bone of good quality carried right down to the feet, which are round and strong. The **stifle** not too straight or too bent, and the dog neither cow-hocked nor moving too wide behind. The dog must stand and move true all round on legs and feet, with toes close and well arched, the soles being thick and strong, and when the dog is in full coat the limbs should be well feathered. **Coat :** Dense, of fine quality and texture, flat as possible. **Colour :** Black or liver. **General :** A bright, active dog of medium size (weighing from 60 lb. to 70 lb.) with an intelligent expression, showing power without lumber and raciness without weediness.

THE FLAT-COATED RETRIEVER

Origin and History.—Down to the beginning of the present century the flat-coated retriever, originally known as the wavy-coated, held undisputed sway alike in the field and on the show bench. By that time he had been bred to a high degree of perfection, thanks to a large extent to the exertions and enthusiasm of the late Mr. S. E. Shirley of Ettington, Warwickshire. This gentleman, whose name will always be remembered with respect as the founder of the Kennel Club in 1873, was largely responsible for laying the foundations of the variety on a solid basis. The material with which he had to work first was vastly different from that known to us. He began by trying to get rid of the conspicuous faults that were attributable to the Newfoundland, and to get a flat coat instead of a wavy. In order to do this, it is supposed that he resorted to collie blood.

In the course of time the Shirley strain became so ubiquitous that he had the greatest difficulty in finding new blood. He was seconded in his efforts by a number of able sporting men, and in the dying years of the old century, flat-coated retrievers were among the most popular of the show dogs. They were in so much demand that the best earned small fortunes at stud. Mr. L. Allen Shuter's *Ch. Darenth* is said to have enriched him to the extent of £1,400, without reckoning the value of his services in his own kennels. I have also a note

FLAT-COATED RETRIEVER : Champion *Tosca British Maid*, the property of Mr. R. H. Upton of 13 Groby Road, Chorlton-cum-Hardy, Manchester.

to the effect that his son, *Horton Rector*, had made £1,300 when he was still in his prime. I shall not attempt to mention the names of all those who have been conspicuously associated with the variety, but it will not be invidious to place on record that Mr. H. Reginald Cooke started his *Riverside* strain some fifty years ago with stock bought from Mr. Shirley. He also gave two hundred guineas for *High Legh Blarney*, who came into the market on the death of Lieut.-Colonel Cornwall-Legh. *Blarney*, who died in 1913 at the age of eleven, was never beaten, and his services at the stud were so much in demand that he had paid for his cost inside of two years.

Standard Description.—The standard formulated by the Flat-coated Retriever Association aims at: " a bright active dog of medium size (weighing from 60 lb. to 70 lb.) with an intelligent expression, showing power without lumber and raciness without weediness." **Head.**—The head is long and nicely moulded, skull flat and moderately broad, a slight stop between the eyes; eyes of medium size, dark brown or hazel; jaws long and strong, ears small and well set on close to the sides of the head. **Body.**—The neck should be long and free from throatiness, set symmetrically and placed obliquely in shoulders; chest deep and fairly broad with a well-defined brisket on which the elbows should work cleanly and evenly. Foreribs should be fairly flat, showing a gradual spring, well-arched in the centre of the body but rather lighter towards the quarters; back short, square and well-ribbed-up, with muscular quarters; stern short, straight and well set on, carried gaily but not very much above the level of the back. *Legs and Feet.*—The forelegs should be perfectly straight, with bone of good quality carried right down to the feet, which should be round and strong; stifle neither too straight nor too bent. **Coat.**—The coat should be dense, of fine quality in texture, as flat as possible. **Colour.**—The colour may be black or liver. Apparently in recent times some of the sterns have been getting too long, for from time to time suspicions have been entertained that the removal of a joint or two is not altogether a thing unknown.

THE FLAT-COATED RETRIEVER

At one period the Flat-Coated Retriever was known as the Wavy, but the present title more justifies the coat, and is therefore suitable. The improvements made with firearms, and the system adopted later of driving birds up to the gun, compelled sportsmen to produce a type of dog that was not too hard in mouth, and not only had a good nose, but was capable of swimming upstream with a wounded bird. He also must have the strength to carry a hare, and last, but by no means least, the intelligence and traits necessary with a gun-dog.

In all these the Flat-Coated Retriever has come up to expectations, and gained a position which he is capable of upholding. These dogs are presumed to be the result of outcrossing the Newfoundland with the English setter and pointer, and the late Mr. Shirley, founder of

the English Kennel Club, with the assistance of Colonel Cornwall Leigh
and Mr. Shuter, did much to get the breed stabilised as we know it
today.

The coat should be abundant and close, and long enough to fall
in gentle and regular waves, the hair being a glossy jet-black, and free
from brindles, tan or white markings, although a few white hairs are
occasionally found on the chest. Their backs, loins, and hind-quarters
should, without positive heaviness, be strong; feet moderate in size,

FLAT COATED RETRIEVER

compact and with hard soles, and the interstices between the toes pro-
tected with hair. The stern should be strong and carried gay, but not
curled over the back; the neck rather long and muscular, with a supple
appearance. The eyes should be mild in expression, dark in colour, and
large; the ears small, set on well back and low, free from fringe, but
covered with soft silky hair. The head should be for the size of the
animal large and long, with a good development of brain before the
ears; the muzzle should be long and rather square, with a capacious
mouth and good level teeth.

CANINE HISTORY.
Here is Mr. L. Allen Shuter's famous dog, "Darenth", which played so great a part in improving the breed of Retrievers.

FLAT-COATED RETRIEVER.
Mr. Allen Shuter's Ch. "Horton Rector", the sire of Mr. H. Reginald Cooke's
Ch. "Grouse of Riverside", a winner of the St. Neots Open Stakes.

Photo]   [E. C Reid.

AN OLDER TYPE.

Here indeed is a very remarkable type of Retriever, suggesting its Newfoundland ancestry, with the coat then known as
"wavy-coated" but now commonly termed "flat-coated"

CH. "WORSLEY BESS".

Another noted Flat-Coated Retriever of the days before the development of the narrow head. "Bess" was the property of Mr. Reginald Cooke. (From a painting by Maud Earl.)

Flat-Coated Retriever.—This member of the Retriever group was originally known as the "Wavy-Coated Retriever", by reason of its jacket showing what is termed by the fair "a permanent marcel wave". But as the variety progressed, so did the coat "flatten out", until at last the original denomination was abandoned in favour of that by which this dog is now known.

There can hardly be a doubt as to the origin of the Flat-Coated Retriever—and, incidentally, of that of the Labrador—both breeds having been evolved from the same source · namely, the Lesser Newfoundland dog, and, in some cases, from the smaller dog of Chesapeake Bay.

The lumber ships plying between St. John's and various British ports used to bring with them dogs of these types, for which they found a ready market; especially among gamekeepers, who imagined—and rightly too—that they would make excellent housedogs and efficient bodyguards when their masters were on night duty and poachers were on the prowl.

But they soon discovered that these animals possessed remarkable scenting powers; were very keen on game and were amenable to discipline. But they were heavily built and cumbersome, and not as well balanced as might be desired.

Some of these gamekeepers, therefore, started to improve matters by crossing these imported dogs with various gun-dogs.

DASH OF RIVERSIDE"

It is no wonder that this breed became so popular. Mr. H. Reginald Cooke's beautiful dog.

ONE OF THE OLD TYPE.

Some say that these powerfully built Flat-Coated Retrievers were too heavy and prefer the more lightly built dog of to-day.

CH. "HIGH LEGH BLARNEY".

One of the most famous of all Flat-Coated Retrievers, owned by Mr. H. Reginald Cooke. The painting by Maud Earl is one of her finest works. It shows "Blarney" holding a grouse.

Matings with Spaniels were not as successful as had been hoped, so resort was had to Pointers and Setters. The desire was to preserve the black coat as being more suitable than any other. In the issue thus produced, were types more or less constant, which respectively provided the nucleus of the Labrador (where a Pointer was used) ; and that of the Wiry or Flat-Coated Retriever (where the Setter cross has been resorted to).

A fair number of the original members of the family bred, as above described, were scattered

Kennel Club, of which he became the first President and Chairman of Committee.

Having an unbounded faith in the merit of "Zelstone"—as proved in the field and in the dog's prospects as a sire—his owner gathered together a select kennel of matrons and began at once to breed a strain of Flat-Coated Retrievers which held its own with the gun, or on the show bench, for many years.

From one of these bitches was produced "Moonstone", a dog which stood out from all his

Photo]   [Sport and General

AT FLAT-COATED RETRIEVER TRIALS

Major H. L. A. Swann's 'Kennett Ruth", having retrieved the game that has fallen on the other side of the road, returns with it to the guns in the spinney   Roads are often a nuisance on shooting days because of the crowd likely to collect as sightseers.

about in districts adjacent to the ports entered by the lumber ships, which had introduced the original Newfoundland stock ; but it was some time before these were recognized as a separate breed. The first dog to attract individual notice was one "Ben", but evidence of his having been successfully exhibited is wanting.

Nevertheless, this dog was—if such chronicles as are available are accurate—the sire of "Zelstone" a dog which lovers of the breed have universally accepted as the "Adam" of the established breed.

He was the property of the late Sewallis Evelyn Shirley, of Ettington Park, Stratford-on-Avon (at one time Conservative Member for Co. Monaghan). who was mainly instrumental in founding the

contemporaries in point of quality symmetry balance, action and type.

The writer awarded the highest honours to "Moonstone" when, as a puppy, he made his *début* at the Kennel Club's show at the Crystal Palace. This was the first of "Moonstone's" successes, but not the last ; for he went from triumph to triumph. and, indeed, was never beaten on the show bench. Moreover, he had the reputation of being invaluable to the gun, with the physical advantages commensurate with his executive ability. At stud. too, he proved himself an outstanding success. Probably the pedigree of every champion of the breed to-day, as in the past, can be traced, either in tail male or female, to "the immortal Moonstone".

Photo]   [Sport and General.

WATERFOWL.

Retrievers are excellent workers both on land and in water. Like most dogs, they are powerful swimmers and use their brains. Above is seen a Flat-Coated type retrieving from a pond.

Photo]   [Sport and General.

BY THE POND.

Wounded wild fowl will sometimes hide away amongst the reeds and rushes, or may even remain below the water, hoping to escape detection. Perhaps just the tip of their beaks may be seen above the surface. Above, a Flat-Coated Retriever recovers the "shot".

It was one of "Sloe's" offspring which was the first bearer of the "Black" distinction. An unfriendly cat had deprived this "Black Cloth" (as he was named) of his left eye ; but, even so, he was deemed good enough to win "first and challenge prize" at Birmingham, and, moreover, eventually he annexed Championship honours.

But it was his son, "Black Drake", which became such a power in Flat-Coated Retriever circles ; whereby hangs a story which is worth recording. "Black Cloth's" owner, having come across a particularly impressive bitch, whose pedigree went back to "Zelstone", without any intermediate in-breeding, arranged with her owner a union with Ch. "Black Cloth". In the event of success, the former was to have first choice of puppies, the latter second choice, and so on alternately.

In due course there were seven whelps, of which one appeared to be more hearty and promising than the rest, so this unit entered the "Black" kennels and became known as "Black Drake".

Another of the same litter passed to Mr. Reginald Cooke. This was a smaller puppy, but of exquisite quality, and one which eventually proved himself to be the best of the breed that had appeared since the days of "Moonstone". Up to now,

A SNAPSHOT

Heads of two Flat-Coated Retrievers that have been sired by "Boy of Riverside" (dam unknown). Sent by Miss M. Wood, an entrant to our photographic competition.

the "Blacks" had been predominant, and had practically swept the boards at the leading shows. But when "Black Drake" and "Wimpole Peter" (as Mr. Cooke's puppy had been named) met at Cruft's, the "Black" flag was lowered, and "Drake's" litter brother held the trump card for some years. In fact he, and he only, stood in the way of his bigger brother ever becoming a full champion. "Black Drake", although (on this occasion) beaten on the bench, became a sire of outstanding brilliance.

His services were in constant demand throughout the length and breadth of the land. No matter what the quality or antecedents of his succession of mates, each produced at least one offspring which took high honours on the bench or in the field. Often, every whelp in the litter became a prize-winner. On the other hand, "Wimpole Peter" was a comparative failure at stud, for he never succeeded in siring anything which approached his own high quality.

But Mr. Cooke's kennel flourished, and for a time was a serious menace to the position erstwhile occupied by the "Blacks". Then, joining in the fray, came Colonel Legh, of Legh Hall, Mr. Vincent Davies, and others, among whom were many enterprising and intelligent gamekeepers, who gallantly supported the breed, then enjoying its halcyon days and popular favour. But the same invaluable "Ettington blood" still ran in the veins of each of the ruling lights of the Flat-Coated Retriever coterie.

Then certain breeders came to the conclusion that the foreface

Photo]   [Keystone

STRANGE, BUT TRUE.

"Fanny", a Flat-Coated Retriever belonging to Mr. J. Smart, of Rossie, Fifeshire, has developed a great fondness for its master's ferrets, frequently carrying them about. They do not seem to mind the unusual method of transport.

[Photo]   [Fall.

A HANDSOME QUARTET.

Miss Phizackles with four of her "Atherbram" Retrievers, all of which are prize winners.   The three in front appear to be of exceptionally good type.   Whereas until recently women breeders did not go in for large dogs, to-day they do so to a considerable extent, and are holding their own against the sterner sex, who once had the monopoly in this field.

and jaws of the Flat-Coated Retrievers were too short to enable them to retrieve a hare or a pheasant in style and comfort. With this view in mind they tried to lengthen the face by introducing Borzoi blood to their polyglot Flat-Coats; the pedigrees of which contained names foreign to the hitherto jealously guarded Ettington records.

The products immediately displayed narrow skulls and long forefaces, giving to the whole head a "coffin-like" structure and aspect.

The old-established judges were unwilling to recognize this new type, but in time the resistance broke down. New judges took the place of the old, and the Flat-Coated Retriever became a breed with long narrow heads and weak muzzles. Some "old-time" breeders and exhibitors gave up the breed altogether, but a few held on and eventually succeeded in putting the "coffin-headed" dogs in their proper place, "below the salt"!

But the damage had been done, and it took generations of careful breeding to eliminate the traces of this destructive experiment; to which also is attributed, by many, the decline in the popularity of the Flat-Coated variety, and the apotheosis of the Labrador.

But in 1932, at Cruft's, it seemed as though a recovery was approaching, for an entry of over one hundred and seventy was secured, but unfortunately this betterment did not continue and failed to be progressive.

At the ensuing Kennel Club's Show at the Crystal Palace there were only nine entries, though the appointed judge was an expert of high repute. This falling off was inexplicable, and the early extinction of the "Flat-Coat" as a breed was sadly prophesied. It was not until "Cruft's 1934" came round, with the writer (who had officiated two years previously) again sporting "the judicial badge", that yet another welcome resuscitation of the "Flat-Coat" was manifested. A fine entry—distinguished by both quantity and quality—giving promise of renewal of the popularity of one of the most beautiful, intelligent, and loyal and affectionate of all our resplendent gun-dog breeds.

DESCRIPTION OF THE FLAT-COATED RETRIEVER.

GENERAL.—A dog of moderate size, somewhat of the Setter type (especially that of the Red Irish Setter) with liberty and length; though as regards the latter, it is more suggestive than actual, for the measurement from the point of the withers to the "set on" of the "flag" or stern is (where a typical unit is concerned) the same as the former point to the ground.

Note.—This measurement also holds good as regards the Labrador; though at first glance the latter appears to be much squarer and shorter in the back than the Flat-Coat. The height at the shoulder of the latter is about 23–25 ins. in dogs, and 19–22 ins. in bitches.

COLOUR. — Usually a whole black. A small star of white on the chest is permissible; but white on the limbs or head is fatal.

Note. — Chocolate-coloured puppies often appear in litters, the parents of which are of the orthodox black hue. Such are eligible to compete on equal terms with their own kin. It is difficult to account for this variation, but it is apparently a hereditary peculiarity, and is evidently due to some mysterious atavistic influence.

It is a strange thing that though these chocolate-tinted Flat-Coats are of fairly common occurrence, no other colour is to be met with in the breeding of this Retriever. The mating of black Labradors, whose immediate parents and forebears were of the same hue, often results in the production of yellow, golden, or almost white stock, but seldom, if ever, chocolate. This would seem to

Photo] *[Fall.*

"STAINTON SPINNER".

Mr. T. H. Moorby specializes in sporting dogs, and the dog shown above is a soundly built youngster from his kennel, and is of a type that may be expected to do well both in the field and on the bench.

Photo] *[Fall*

"BETTY OF RIVERSIDE".

The name "Riverside" stands for some of the very best in Flat-Coated Retrievers, referring as it does to Mr. H. Reginald Cooke, one of the leading breeders and authorities on the breed.

suggest that some of the original dogs of the North-West, which were mated with British Pointers, were of the Chesapeake Bay variety, individuals of which are frequently yellow or golden.

POINTS OF CONFORMATION.

HEAD.—This should be of fair length. The skull flat on top and moderately broad between the ears, which are of fair length and falling closely to the cheek. When extended, the tips should reach to the outer corner of the eye. The cheek itself should be flush and not showing undue prominence of the cheek-bones. The foreface of moderate length. The length from the occiput to the inner corner of the eye should be the same as from the latter point to the end of the nose, which should be of fair size, a deep black, with fairly open nostrils. Jaw, strong and perfectly level, with the lips and flews well braced; teeth strong and white; eyes placed rather wide small, but not too deep-set. A round, pedunculated (i.e. prominent) eye is very undesirable. The colour of the iris is a deep, rich brown, but not sloe-black! Its expression should be highly intelligent and altogether affectionate and benevolent. A light eye is objectionable. a yellow one fatal!

NECK.—Fairly long and well moulded; set symmetrically into oblique shoulders which are not overloaded with muscle. and which work with piston-like and rhythmic regularity.

CHEST.—Moderately broad and forming a deep brisket, on which the legs, in action, impinge.

FORE RIBS.—Strong, and only slightly rounded.

BACK RIBS.—Rather more "sprung", but not "barrel-like"; and well "ribbed-up".

COUPLINGS.—(I.e. the space between the last back rib and the stifle) should be of not more than three or four inches in measurement. "Open" couplings are highly objectionable. The stifle itself well bent.

BACK.—Strong and level, nicely rounded at the quarters, which are powerful and well muscled in the thighs, second thighs and gaskins.

HOCKS.—Bony; fairly bent and comparatively close to the ground.

TAIL, "STERN" or "FLAG".—Of moderate length (from "set on" to point of hock) and well feathered. A long "flag", curling or "ringing" at the extremity, is a terrible disfigurement. Where it exists, the temptation to curtail it is acute, and many owners have transgressed a rule which, in the main, is well justified. Detection of such mutilation entails disqualification of both dog and exhibitor. The flag should be carried gaily, on a level with the back.

LEGS.—Straight, with plenty of bone, which is carried down to the feet; the knees of fair size, flat and neither "standing over" nor "back"; the pasterns strong, but springy enough to "give play" when the dog is "pulling up", or "on the turn".

FEET.—Large; the toes close and well knuckled up; but they, too, should be pliant enough to spread suddenly when required to do so, as is often the case where the dog is sent to retrieve a wounded, but still active, hare or rabbit. or a "jiggering" pheasant or partridge.

COAT.—Smooth and fine, but showing a denser under-coat. It should be glossy and rather soft to the touch, but not silky. Nothing shows up that indefinable and desirable attribute "quality" in a Flat-Coated Retriever more resplendently than a coat which is diligently well-groomed and "strapped" until it catches the high lights.